The Man Alone

Acknowledgments

Many thanks to Peterloo Poets for permission to reprint the poems from *Thinking of Happiness*.

Also to the editors of *Areté*, *automatic lighthouse*, *The North*, *Seam*, *Signs and Humours: The Poetry of Medicine* (Calouste Gulbenkian Foundation), *The Reader*, *The Rialto* and *The Wolf* who first published some of the new poems.

Also by Michael Laskey:

Cloves of Garlic (Smith/Doorstop Books, 1989)
Thinking of Happiness (Peterloo Poets, 1991)
In the Fruit Cage (Smith/Doorstop Books, 1997)
The Tightrope Wedding (Smith/Doorstop Books, 1999)
Permission to Breathe (Smith/Doorstop Books, 2004)
Living by the Sea (Smith/Doorstop Books, 2007)

The Man Alone

New & Selected Poems

Michael Laskey

Smith/Doorstop Books

Published 2008 by
Smith/Doorstop Books
The Poetry Business
Bank Street Arts
32-40 Bank Street
Sheffield S1 2DS

ISBN 978-1-906613-29-7
Michael Laskey hereby asserts his moral right to be identified
as the author of this book.

British Library Cataloguing-in-Publication Data. A catalogue
record for this book is available from the British Library.

Designed & typeset by Utter
Printed & bound by Lightning Source
Author's photograph by Claire McNamee
Cover painting: People on the Beach (August for the People)
1951 by Michael Andrews

Distributed by Central Books Ltd., 99 Wallis Road,
London E9 5LN

The Poetry Business gratefully acknowledges the help of Arts
Council England.

Supported by
ARTS COUNCIL
ENGLAND

Contents

Thinking of Happiness

The Tightrope Wedding

Permission to Breathe

New Poems

Thinking of Happiness

On the Anniversary of V.E. Day 1985

After the speeches, the solemn faces,
the muted melancholic brass,
once more silence.

I still don't know what my father thought
feeling his Lancaster lifting off
into the huge cockpit of night.

Or Uncle Len, injured, I know
only by hearsay, at Mount Cassino –
the wound didn't show.

They both survived to find me fat
on my mother's lap. Killers,
victims, my first real men.

But they wouldn't speak of what they'd done
or had done to them;
they held their peace

and hold it still,
remarkable as this pill-box standing
out in the currents of corn.

Meeting our Father

Almost unbearable having to wait
and wait in the terminal building
checking all-comers. A year it had been –
his job, mum said – but we knew him at once –
his features varnished – and raced to be first
at his side and allowed to uncover the budgie:
a fearful clatter of wings. Lupin.
Not used to us yet. And though we began
teaching him carols on the way home,
his cage balanced on our bare knees,
we soon went quiet, seeing how silly
our hopes had been. And he never spoke,
though he'd settle on my head while I did my prep
and lived with us years after Dad had left.

Letters from my Mother

Roughly once a month
in prompt response to mine
her envelopes arrive:

loyal to her brand
of stationery, her firm
rounded hand unchanged.

Through my unsettled years
of doors she never saw
and views she couldn't share

she's kept it up, composed
God only knows what quires
of cheerful humdrum prose.

Like this one, bland with facts,
with golf, gardening, weather
and names of those who came:

eight sides of unevent-
ful life with what went on
inside her head left out

as if of no account.
The same dear selfless door.
No hint that she's afraid
it's cancer.

Fishing for Mackerel

for Mike Curtis

On all that wide water he and I
dispersed along flightpaths of birds flocking
across the unfenced fields of sky
and we wheeled freely back to the rocking
boat with its wake running straight to Cley
and our talk overlapping, interlocking,

till at length I asked 'Where's the rod and reel?
And what bait do they take, these mackerel?'
and Curt, startled by my revealed
ignorance, drew from the cluttered well
of the boat hand-lines which he unpeeled,
each one barbed at tactical

intervals with a dozen steel
hooks and vividly coloured feathers:
fast food with mackerel appeal.
So we dropped our lines down into that nether
world looming up underneath our keel
and sat back to wait together.

And if I was sceptical, if I was never
to catch a mackerel, what the hell?
If this was fishing, then no endeavour
had ever suited me half as well,
with half a mind on the hand's light tether
riding with Curt on the slow sea swell,

till this spell of content tensed, shattered
at a yank from below, a simultaneous yell
of delight from Curt as the shoal battered
by and we gathered our catch up into the bell
of the air, their tails gonging like clappers,
immaculate, miraculous mackerel:

not one at a time, but four or five
jangling my line, as the shoal without number
or interruption still arrived
and, while I was fumbling, would have passed under
our bows and vanished, had not Curt, alive
to my flapping, expertly unencumbered

his line and mine and flung them back
and, before I'd even half-grasped my luck
or my thankfulness, more fish snatched
at our hooks; and although we must have struck
and singled them out, yet we too were their catch,
clutched by their bubbling life bursting up.

When I think of happiness, I think of that.

A Change of Clothes

Always I knew there'd been knitted rugs
pat on the lino in my parents' room:
punts to push off on or stepping stones
I could change on a whim, to frighten myself,
into crocodiles. The cane-seated chair
had always been there, right-angled, handily
placed for my climb up the bed's sheer face
and onto the plateau of Saturday morning,
when the world moved over and let me in.
There under the Heath, next door to the station –
Gospel Oak – and close to the shops
at South End Green, what more could I want?

Not school – not learning my name was odd;
or having Steve Lawrence ask why my Dad
and Mum spoke funny; or under their bed
one wet afternoon finding the case
carefully packed: a change of clothes
even for me, some papers in English
and some in a language that had to be Polish,
and right at the bottom a wallet containing
£25 that over the years,
needing this and that, I gradually spent,
each time really meaning to pay it all back.

A Charm for Maurice

Only just arrived, only just alive,
a bare kilo for special care,
premature baby boy grown man
in more minds than mine, gramme by gramme
add weight to hopes we hardly dare
breathe for a future where you'll thrive

unfussed, unfêted, undiscussed
for days on end, where you can sleep
heavily in your room next door
to Graham and Tanya, or peel and core
their apple of sleep with your most sweet
incisive cries – if you must.

But now in an incubator, fed through the nose,
shielded by perspex, by nurses, by prayer,
Thursday's child, with so far to go
to wear your folded baby clothes,
journey to the threshold of fresh air,
outgrowing this poem and putting on prose.

The Fancy

Glanced out this lunchtime and saw old Threadkell
coming home, his rusty blue van
turning into the lane opposite,
a neighbour of mine I consider
                    hardly at all;

as he'll still walk by me not meeting
my eye, not even slightly inclining
his head. But whether he disapproves
of me particularly or would withhold
                    recognition

indifferently from anyone living
opposite him for a mere six years
I don't know. Perfect love would be to care
for him like air, enlivening the brick
                    wall of his face

unnoticed, without ulterior motives.
Imperfectly I try to imagine
I'm an unsmiling, early rising, gruff,
tough, retired agricultural worker
                    and widower

like Jack Threadkell, wedded to a treadmill
of practical tasks: tending slow vegetables;
cooped up with hens and the more unlikely
sprightly bantams he breeds for the fancy;
                    then off somewhere

with his chain-saw slung in the back of the van
among the muscular clutter of tools
he knows how to use. And now home for dinner.
I watch him drive in, hear the engine die,
        the van-door slam.

Staring out blankly I feel my features
worked quickly, reshaped to fit a new face:
it's his dead wife seizing her chance to peer
out through my eyes, soothed to catch sight of him
        looking so well.

Weekends

for Ben Horwood at forty

Returning your Joe, at what would have been dusk
but for the snow: with a one-track mind
on the tightrope road, driving slowly

and, despite packed ice and Joe's distracting
narrative eccentricities, we
arrived at the gate as you stepped out:

not content with an afternoon spent
skating, but now going, racing the dark,
up Bramblebush with the older two

for a quick sledge, pulling behind you
The Flexible Flyer – wood and metal
fast together these forty years.

I turned and drove alone through the given
weather, steadied by the thought of you, Ben,
plunging down into Sunday's last hollow.

Firelighters

for Lesley

Soon after he left you, another first:
entering the cold husk of the house
with two tired children you know the worst
has happened, the Parkray has gone out

and find yourself kneeling without thinking
without faith before the boiler,
riddling briskly, cinders and clinker
cleared, the grate a waiting void

which he'd have filled with his unhurried
origami, a fan of spills
pinched round compact coils and buried
under kindling, chips of coal.

Always miraculous that phoenix,
now extinguished. But all you need's
to hand: a screwed up man-size Kleenex,
a firelighter, some sticks and a hod

of coal to feed a single match.
Nothing to it. You lift the flap
for draught, adjust the thermostat
and feel warmth slowly welling up.

Between Two Lit Rooms

After work, for once, to walk home,
not to drive, foot hinged to the clutch,
through town, but to walk on your own
out into the open dark,

the Plough, the Pole Star, Orion
distancing you from your day.
Then down the ringing wrought-iron
spiral staircase to the softer

asphalt of the all but empty
car park. One January night.
Such space around you, such plenty:
a good fifteen minutes walking

between two lit rooms, the split halves
of your life, the future, the past.
But for now a skive down this path,
the ridge of the fence furred with frost.

Family Planning

We called you Jenny after the girl
who kissed Leigh Hunt, at once foresaw
how soon I'd bore you with his poem.

But after all you'll never know it:
no more children, we've agreed –
both being free and forced to choose.

Your three brothers, who brushed in turn
past your inapplicable name,
must go on growing up alone:

unmoved by the pull of their own
new moon, unrocked by a small
tyrannical sister. Our Jenny.

Nothing but a word; familiar
features resolutely blurred;
but the lips ineffably soft.

Registers

Out of the warm primordial cave
of our conversations, Jack's gone.
No more chit-chat under the blankets
pegged over chairs and nipped in drawers.

Throughout his first five years an ear
always open, at worst ajar,
I catch myself still listening out
for sounds of him in the sensible house

where nothing stirs but the washing machine
which clicks and churns. I'm loosening his arms
clasped round my neck, detaching myself
from his soft protracted kiss goodbye.

Good boy, diminishing down the long
corridors into the huge unknown
assembly hail, each word strange,
even his name on Miss Cracknell's tongue.

Living with the Doctor

Once a week I suppose, like a white
wash or my cauliflower bake,
somebody living here dies;

and even if you don't go,
if it's not your day on call
or if you're away, you'll know

in the end: the others will usually
say or someone'll send you a form
if it happens in hospital.

Sometimes you tell me, name names
you think may ring bells for me –
Elsie Fairweather, old Billy Sore –

and sometimes you don't: you come in
bearing dry clothes from the line
which you fold while I'm dishing up lunch.

But on days you need to make sense
of an accident or to relax
the grip of a grief, then we speak

of who and how, what you could do
to help. We've had to develop
a voice that can cope with death

properly, yet fit it in
over our bowls of soup,
before we're summoned to watch

Jack's magic or unsnarl Ben's maths.
Privileged knowledge for me –
a broadening, a warning –

but for you I'm not so sure
this morning, finding your clothes
in a heap on the bathroom floor

and knowing you must have been out
on a call in the night. The jabbing
phone; your questions; our duvet

closing behind you; your footsteps:
I slept through them all, insensible
even to your shivering return.

On the A12

Towards the end of a long drive home,
your nervous system subdued by pistons,
your children, gone through the quarrelsome

miles, mild now in the back of your mind,
and the road once more your own, the known
camber of a bend, horizons, signs

you read for the sake of their refreshed
welcoming names, not to tick them off,
Ufford, Hacheston, Campsey Ash.

And it's almost over, you're all but back
unpacking, when for a sudden split
second the road, that must know the make

and colour of your car and your number plate,
turns towards your returning smile
a quite blank unfamiliar face

so out of place you can't remember
where in the wheeling world you are
or what time it is of what day, month, year.

Living with a Death

for my wife's mother

1.
These ceremonies, Gee, to mark
your death, two hundred miles away
from us, though with your girls, today:

for Jack and me a sweet unique
after breakfast hour of sleep
that creased our clothes but soothed our souls;

between the sandpit and the swings
a comma in mid-afternoon,
its ragged wings in perfect tune;

to fetch the older boys from school
a borrowed dormobile, a slow
heightened ride round our known roads;

then sherry in your memory
and nuts they did their best to share
lovingly with you not here.

I think you know it all, our tears
and Ben and Tim asleep upstairs
for comfort in a single bed.

2.
What I remember best is this:
the wonderful heaviness of your head
on my shoulder where you'd fallen asleep
for the first time. Whatever was said
was as nothing to that.

Though all you meant
was a warm on the bed, a breather, a break
from the rigours of revision, the cold

afternoon laid the blankets of dusk
so imperceptibly over us
                      that you slept on
undisturbed and I, far too elated
to sleep, still shouldered the weight of your trust.

So tonight lay down your boulder of grief
let it ache in the same old feeling place.

3.
On Thorpeness beach – where he saw her last,
and most, in the three light years their lives
overlapped – out for a walk,

a winter walk, our boots making blunt
dents in the pebbles, felicitous prints
in a narrow strip of blank new sand.

With her four months dead he hopes she still
remembers us. Leaving these tracks,
these vestiges on Thorpeness beach.

4.
Your face turned away into shadow:
it's your dead mother, dishevelled,
fossicking about in the cellar
after the Scrabble you casually
smuggled out, years back.

But pleased to be called up, released
from amnesia – those cobwebs,

the damp – she picks her fastidious
way up the steps and appears
in the doorway, the daylight, delighted

you've arrived. And now comes alive
receiving you, free to speak
again after weeks on her own,
excusing her hair, the dust
brushed off her skirt and the Scrabble

still inexplicably lost.
As she lists the places she's looked
we're nodding, our eyes not meeting,
not daring to speak, but shaking
with spasms of laughter and grief.

5.
In the deep night Jack cried out
and woke me. What was the matter?

Plainly from his dream he spoke:
'Gee's only got one cover.'

Gee, his eighteen-month-dead
grandmother.

I fetch him a drink and stroke
his snug five-year-old head.

Small wonder she wants to be heard,
mourned, not settled forever

under thick blankets of years.

Laying the Fire

This is the way I deal with the news,
on my knees screwing up page after page
of the Guardians I hardly ever read
otherwise. To fill the grate it only takes
five double sheets, each one unpeeled
and crumpled up rapidly into a ball,
and, in between, time on my hands to read
anything eye-catching, headlines, this
girl of fourteen on a day return
from Durham, dazed by her concert, distressed
at not knowing which way to go for Kings Cross,
but not guessing, now she was guided by him,
how soon she'd be unforgettably lost.
Oh, as they were passing the door of his flat
they had to look in, he said, pick something up;
and once they were safely inside he wasted
no time: raped her, raped her, repeatedly
raped her until he lay limp, at last fell asleep
and she crept out through his open mouth
into the dark hollow of the street
needing help, healing, amnesia,
anger, but not this pair in a car cruising,
who caught her full in their lights – some wild
young slut appealing to them to stop,
asking for it. The end. That was the end
of the story. Another page screwed up,
paper ablaze, blackening, collapsing
under the weight of twigs, sticks, logs
laid in the hearth, gone up in smoke.

Life after Death

After he died he went on speaking
on the ansaphone: he'd apologise
for being out and ask us to leave
our names and messages after the tone.

At first we couldn't, we just hung up,
but steeled ourselves; it was her grief,
her tape that she was perfectly free
not to choose to erase in those early days.

At last though the voice did change to hers
and we were consoled, we found we could breathe
our nonsense into her solemn machine
once more and pictured her smiling, unwinding.

Later we raised it – macabre was the word
we used – and she laughed, told us the truth
was more ordinary than that:
just not knowing how to record herself.

Cucumber

smiles on us too.
From its Latin root
cucumis creeps
through the centuries,
texture and taste
reaching us almost
unchanged, answering
to all but the same name.

Cucumber:
the levity of language
to settle on a word
so mimetic,
cylindrical,
weighty and long,
of a ludicrous
bent like the fruit.

Cucumber:
a licence for staid
middle-aged men
out shopping,
like this one
prodding his son
in the back
with a cucumber gun.

Cucumber
cut for us, bleeds
minute plasma beads;

shows us its useless
rose windows,
its needless number
of seeds. Sixth proof
that God exists:

Cucumber.

The Tightrope Wedding

Home Movies

By the final frame of the film, before
the tinny rattle of a jerked reel
or that dazzle on the bald sitting-room wall,
Dad had leaped up beside the projector

and flicked the switch, so their shaky story
went ratcheting on, only backwards now:
led in by balloons, bouncing cans and clouds
of exhaust, the car came reversing surely

far too fast at the horseshoe of guests
crowding Gran's gravel, and we had to laugh
at the way our would-be father muffed
his entrance, emerging bottom first

to pose for a moment with his right arm
flung round an untarnished version of Mum.
No sound, just a pan of everyone
cracking up, the storm before the calm

delivery by Dad of some old joke.
Hilarious how they all skedaddled
backwards up the steps into the middle
of the reception: a piece of cake

that a waitress snatched; each hopeful wish
promptly returning unopened to sender
as the knife they were forcing up together
lifted off, leaving the icing unblemished;

a quick balancing trick put the tiers in place;
then unedited longueurs – little movement,
too many self-conscious close-ups of distant
relations and friends they'd lost without trace

and whom we'd never known – nothing comical
except for a slim-line uncle Jim
brightening as glass after glass of his wine
vanished, sucked up by the mouth of the bottle.

It was round about then, while we were all
full of it, paralytic at him
sobering up, that Mum left the room
with a kind of abruptness that niggled

(or would have, if we'd adjusted our focus,
not chosen not to notice) and so she missed
what followed: their ceremonial kiss
outside the church; Dad reaching across

to conceal her face with the antique veil;
and once the blinking guests had withdrawn
into the dark doorway arm in arm
he steered her backwards, helped by two small

bridesmaids tugging her train in towards
the vestry, the moment when he'd unscrew
his pen and one by one they'd undo
their signatures, going over the words

from right to left so they disappeared,
and suddenly the twinkle in Dad's eye
was a hard gleam in the flickering light
and the rare warmth of the atmosphere

too close: not one of us raised the ghost
of a laugh as Dad softly eased the ring
off the finger so gladly held out to him,
or dared interrupt to point out the past

was spilling out, already ankle-deep
on the floor and spreading. He stood so still
we didn't exist. There was nothing real
but that slither of negatives at his feet.

Auntie

(1902-1998)

Among the stuff in her room
this album turned up. Slid under
the cellophane on page one
her message: *This book is for Kay*
and here we are, dated, arranged,
on the beach, in front of the Cabin,
the boys wearing clothes I'd forgotten
yet my fingers can still feel the weave
and weight of, tops I could ease
gently over their ears in my sleep.
Here's Jack's green Clothkits tracksuit,
Tim's slinky red shorts, Ben's tough cords.
Our first ten years in Suffolk
when Auntie still drove and came up
with old nursing friends every summer.
Their names are on the tip of my tongue:
Gam. Barbara. Dorothy Menassah
piggybacking Tim over the pebbles.
And Auntie not appearing of course
except on the first and last pages
where she's put herself out of the wind
in the porch with a cup and saucer,
the Cabin's everlasting plain blue.
She'd a soft spot for backs. Here's one
of us pushing our bikes down the slatted
wooden walkway, heading off home.
But whenever she calls we look up
smiling warmly, perfectly natural.

The Last Swim

September, October ... one thing
you don't know at the time is when
you've had your last swim: the weather
may hold, may keep nudging you in.

Only afterwards, sometimes days on,
it dawns on you that you've done:
just the thought of undressing outdoors,
exposing bare skin, makes you wince.

And that's best, to have gone on swimming
easily to the end: your crawl
full of itself, and the future
no further than your folded towel.

The Day After

I made a leek and potato soup
the day after, prompted by the look
of the peeled potato going soft
in a glass of water by the sink.
Beyond the back door, drizzle
and the raw morning air argued for soup,
added their weight to the nod of the knife
slicing the leeks, wrapped up in themselves,
into logs, into rings – whites, yellows and greens –
that I agitated till they came clean
in a bowl of cold water and set
simmering with the potato in stock
I'd thickened with flour, sprinkled with dried
herbs – rosemary, thyme – and startled
with a splash of leftover wine.
We had it for lunch, liquidised
with the top of the milk and heated through
and though I dare say you didn't notice
the taste, you ate it. It's sometimes too soon
to speak about things, but you've got to eat.

Driving Home

You're on your own driving home,
the miles light music that you spool
from wheel to wheel. Each dip and bend
hums with the tune. It's late at night
and, though you're tired, it's not far now:
the glow shows up across the fields.

A thud, a simultaneous crunch,
and, as you stamp on brakes and wrench
hard at the wheel, a scrape, a thump.
The reeling darkness stalls and drops
a lump of terror in your lap.
The car has shuddered to a stop

facing backwards and across,
so what you see is this: lit up
beside the verge, a buckled bike
and in the ditch beyond, a heap
of tangled clothes. Nothing moves.
A country road. No other lights

in sight but yours. And what you think
at once is this: no witnesses.
You're stunned, appalled. What's to be done?
You can't park where you are. Reverse.
Whatever damage to the wing
it's not caved in. The car still steers.

You know it's dangerous to move
some injuries. You hesitate.
You've never been much good with blood.
Still no-one comes. It might make sense
to drive fast to the nearest house
and use their phone. You must fetch help.

The first place – now you think of it
as you slow down – 's a second home:
it looks shut up, hedge overgrown.
The next's for sale. The third's a farm
down a rough track, two fields back,
a cert for early nights, and dogs.

You check your mirror. Up ahead
no looming lights. No traffic still.
The big house on the corner's black
against the sky. A waste of time.
To pull those distant sleepers back
a bell would have to shrill and shrill.

You had no warning, never saw him.
It makes you wonder. You were driving
well, not wildly; you'd remember
any twitch of fright or tightness
on that bend. You would have braked.
What's likely is he had no lights.

One gleaming window seen too late
– already past and going too fast –
makes you dither, lift your foot,
but then the thought that any light
left shining out along this route
might burn for nothing but that bike

settles it. Why knock and call
through bolted doors, unlock alarm
in narrow halls, explain, explain,
when little more than three miles on,
the other side of this small town,
you'll be beside your phone, at home?

The streets are hollow, brightly lit.
A stray dog cocks a leg and sniffs
along a fence. A couple kiss
persistently. A street-lamp blinks.
A van pulls out ahead, turns right
and, unremarked, you roll straight on.

You kill the engine, douse the lights
and sit a moment in the dark
breathing out. Hot metal ticks.
What's done is done. You know a man
who'll fix the car. Softly you close
the up-and-over garage door.

Bike

You, who have borne three sons
of mine, still bear my weight
routinely, transporting me.

An odd pair: your classic spare
lines – elbows, bony frame –
and me, bearlike, cumbersome,

nosing tangled coils of air
you cut through with your pure
purposeful geometry.

With you it's feet off the ground,
a feat passing unremarked
though in full public view.

Keeping each other's balance.
Our talk slow recurrent clicks,
companionable creaks.

Through you I've come to know
winds inside out and raw
weather ignored before;

and nuances of slopes,
the moving earth, green tracks
for blackberries and sloes

for gin, for jam: the tug
and tang of fruit pulling me
clear of the wheel of myself.

Sloes

Our bikes on the verge behind us
bowled over by bush after bush
so lavish with sloes we can't stop
picking them, the powder blue bloom
dissolving wherever we touch
and the glossy black showing through.
They've come a long way from the starry
white flowers they were on bare wood
in the early spring. We roll handfuls
into the plastic bag
I've emptied of spanners and bits
and pieces of puncture repair kits
and turned inside out. Later on
we'll prick them one by one
and steep them in sugar and gin
for months, giving the bottles
a brisk shake every so often.
But for now it's us they're filling,
even to our fingertips stubbed
by pressing phone calls and faxes
they're giving back feeling. I see
your pupils darkening with love.

The Light

At mid-morning seeing the light
in his bedroom still on, the blinds down,
I swear out loud, earmark him
for a piece of my mind. Three hours
it's been on. Three hours since he left
for school and in all that time

I haven't thought of him once.
A tug and the blind rolls up
on itself, admits the dazzle
of days when I ached with love
that I'd point his way as he began
number work, playtime, packed lunch.

The Knife

You brought it with you to the marriage
I think, already in your kitchen drawer
in Savernake Road when we first
pooled our possessions. A perfectly
ordinary kitchen knife: the two
rivets through the dark stained wood
of the handle still holding the blade
firmly after twenty years. Signs
of wear though, as you'd expect: the tip
broken off – used as a lever once
too often – a nick in the edge
and the brown handle mottled, streaked
unevenly where the wood dye's leached.
I like it sharp: gritting my teeth
I grind it between steel wheels
now and again, scare my thumb.
It fits my fist, loves stringing beans,
slicing onions, tomatoes, courgettes.
Who'd have thought it would come to matter
so much to me, this small knife
you say now you're not sure was yours?

Ratatouille

was a revelation, like the simmering
colours of your room that first time:
the purple wall hung with fine
cane blinds; the Indian bedspread;
the cracked basin airing your damp
green flannel; the planks and the bricks
for Lawrence, Sartre, Dostoyevsky,
and others I could see would be
quite beyond me – Gray's Anatomy,
Surgery by Bailey and Love.
I'd never eaten them before
that evening, aubergines. Or courgettes.
Did I even know what they were called?
You unfolded a table and lit
a candle. We sat with our knees
almost touching. Every so often
we paused, forks poised, held our peace
as a train clattered past, shook the glass.
Later on you must have taught me
how to make it, though I still don't get
the chemistry, why salt on the slices
draws out the bitter juices
or why the colours, tastes and textures
blend better, stir me more year by year.

Pudding

For years she tried to get it right,
off and on. No cinnamon,
she learnt, and less vanilla essence.
A pinch of nutmeg, half an ounce
more sugar than it said, not brown –
as she'd used once – but caster.

It was his favourite, so she made it
often and achieved such moistness
in the middle and a skin
so delicate and thickly freckled
he was baffled, just couldn't say
the way his mum's had differed.

At last she'd asked her – it was after
Olga died, when all that sadness
softened them – and she admitted
that what she did was add a little
tin of Ambrosia Creamed Rice.
It's been fresh fruit ever since.

Small Town Life

Mispronounced it probably that first time
I drove through, and had no idea,
not an inkling we'd end up living here.
A hole – mercifully small was the thought
that crossed my mind as it vanished behind.

Cut off for those two days, a perfect
island. The snow had drifted, closed
the schools, disconnected the milk, the post.
We pulled our sledge down the middle of the road,
our heads in the clouds we were breathing out.

Why does it please me so much seeing
these two together and knowing at once
they must be related? It's a resemblance
I never noticed in years of passing them
one at a time: such a nice rhyme.

I know him too, in the bus shelter crew,
a shy boy who'd settle on my knee
in the reading corner, who easily
outstares me now – abashed by his cool
plume of smoke, his bold blank look.

On evenings like this, with November winds
jostling cumulonimbus, the town's
nothing: a ruck of roofs, no-one around,
in the yellow chip shop the television
on its high shelf entertaining itself.

Small enough to walk all the way
round the edge between coffee and lunch.
And never unchanged. Oaks have unclenched.
Tractors make tracks and a lapwing lifts
my head from this heap of sugar-beet.

So now it's you moving. The house,
which I'd thought of simply as yours,
is announcing itself: the For Sale board
clear and inviting. You'll be emptying
shelves soon, striding through hollow rooms.

I consider it too, late at night,
as I do the milk and look east
at the glow the fierce lights broadcast
now over Sizewell: a changed horizon
that proves the town's already moved.

Sometimes at weekends a small lull
comes over the garden and stops
me digging. In the silence far off
I can hear them on the old works field,
yelling hoarsely for a pass, oddly close.

The Jig

Left for the station in plenty
of time. Carried his case for him
through to the platform, insisted on
doing it, and duly swung it
aboard. Then shrugged off his awkward
thanks, squeezed his shoulder and soberly
waved as the train slid forward,
picking up speed, pulling his long
suffering elsewhere. And so I emerged
onto the car park, into the clear
morning air and found my feet
shamelessly dancing a wild little jig.

Hunting the Thimble

We wait in the hall to be called.
Uncle Len gets there first, he jams up
the entrance, poking his head
round the door, asking 'are you quite sure
you're ready now?', eyes all the time
travelling around the room,
while we're shoving him from behind,
protesting, helpless with laughter.
Once we burst in, we begin
glancing high and low, guessing
what it signifies, where whoever's
hidden it has chosen to sit,
watching out for a clue from their eye
movements, and trying to keep track
of the others too, not to miss
any giveaway stillness at the moment
of discovery. But if no-one finds it
at once, we start to settle,
forgetting ourselves as we check
picture-rails, bookshelves, the vaseful
of tulips, the ashen grey tip
of the poker. The sitting-room's
stiff with all of us standing,
our peering heads at odd angles.
But won over by our patient
scrutiny, it slips us a few
suggestions for when it's our go:
that catch on the window, the sockets
round the back of the TV. Not
this time though. Tim's already
sat down with his triple-top smile:
we were looking straight at it before,
but we're cold now, getting colder.

Picking Raspberries with My Mother

So little time left to talk
and arrange things that I must ask her
now when we've hardly begun
picking the raspberries whether
she's thought about what to do
afterwards. She's holding out
the family size Nescafé jar
we're sharing and though I take care
I spill one or two as I funnel
the first handful in, cast down
by my clumsiness. She'll just come home,
she says, turning her attention
back to the canes, not keen
to discuss it. This'll be the last
picking – some are shrivelled already
and the rest, mostly small and pippy,
cling on so the trick is not
to squash them pulling them off.
I gauge the resistance, the give
of each berry between my finger
and thumb, and press on. It's a big
operation, I say, bending down
and peering among leaves and the pricklish
stems I push back. Let's not think
about it, she shudders. But picturing
the tubes she'll sprout, the drip feed,
I clear my throat. She won't be up
to cooking and shopping. She'll need
to go somewhere for convalescence,
a week or two till she can cope.
But she won't be pressed, won't look
beyond the sagging cage, her worry
one jar's not enough for the boys.

We've been working different rows
side by side so I know she's picking
some I wouldn't touch, like that one –
dulled purple, bobbles so soft
they're mush on her fingers she's forced
to flick into the pot. Extra
sweet, she smiles. I bite my tongue.

Home in Suffolk next morning a note
from Tim, who came in too late
for supper with the rest of us:
Delicious raspberries x x x

Doing My Mother's Ironing

My turn now. I spread the board's
awkward legs on the vinyl floor
– sensible dark blue squares
picked out in grey lines
I've never focused on before
in so many years. Like how
exactly you iron, which end
of the shirt you start, perplexed
by tucks, cuffs, sleeves' double ply.
Yet constant, this creak of the pressed
board, the flecked flex scuffing,
the tick of the iron heating up
or cooling, and always the same
smell of hot cotton given off
by this candy-striped blouse
of hers now. Fleshing out
those shadowy movements, I nose
round the buttons, slip a shoulder over
the pointed end and push on,
easing out creases, driving
back and forth to the ward, her worn
smile. She could do with a new cover,
and the mat's shedding flakes of what must
be asbestos. But finished for now
I feel for the catch, need to duck
under to see how it works,
how to stand it upright, this stiff
dancing partner I fold
an arm round and walk to the cupboard
under the stairs where it lives.

The Clothes-peg

How it had happened they neither of them knew
but it only got worse. He hated the blank
blue ice of his stare and she couldn't bear
her thin voice telling him to turn
down the TV please, to stop diddling
with that clothes-peg, which without thinking he
clipped to the hem of her cardigan hanging
over the newel post as he mooched past.
It was Margaret at work who pointed it out
and all day it kept on taking her hand
by surprise, a bump in her cardigan pocket.
So naturally closing his old Noah's Ark
curtains that evening she pegged them together.
A few mornings later it waylaid her
inside her shoe. She snapped it on the end
of his toothbrush handle, so it wouldn't pull through
the holder, and found it next clipping the ear
of Humph, her venerable bear. For him she left it
dangling in the dark from the plastic light pull
in the bathroom, where he lit on the pot
of Paracetamol and dibbled it in.
It felt like a biro caught in his train pass
as he brought it out to show the guard,
and tugging a Kleenex out of the box
she spluttered at the clatter, but said nothing,
just hung it from the lining inside his tie
ready for the morning. And now the drizzle starts
as she's driving to work, she laughs out loud –
lifted by it skimming back and forth
riding on the stalk of the wiper blade.

The Tightrope Wedding

We can't take our eyes off the young
couple walking to meet one another
on this cable strung between twin
towers of the castle. Fifty feet

up in the air and no net. Arms
wide, they're holding out matching
aluminium balancing poles
that are light but so long they bow slightly.

We can see how the slim, dark-haired
and suited groom bends his knees
as he leans forward shifting his weight
onto the front foot to take

his next step. The bride, we assume,
must be doing the same, somehow
holding sway over her stiff
petticoats, the satin and lace;

and, adjusting to any gust
tugging at her train, she comes on
steadily, one white shoe showing,
its soft sole curved over the rope.

They're wired up, they counterbalance
each other, but they're not one flesh yet.
We bite our lips, can't bear to look,
are glad to be distracted

by this tubby, game, down-to-earth priest
about to climb into the picture
up the fire appliance's steep
but not impossible ladder.

Permission to Breathe

The Corpse

He shares my morning cup of tea, likes it
colder than me. Staring at the empty
blue window, he's my dad propped up
glimpsed again through the ward's swing doors.

I reach for my book, find my place
or jump up quick, wash, give myself
a close shave, inhale soap, and froth
the strong teeth he bares at the mirror.

He's a rude child. I rattle him off downstairs,
stop his mouth with muesli, fresh fruit.
Once I'd kiss him goodbye at the school
gates and get on with my life.

But he grows so fast. No time since
he was nothing but a blink in my eye,
a blank at the end of my tunnel,
yet self-evident now, so conspicuous

in the tube some woman stands up
and offers me her seat. Though my feet
are killing me, I decline, my smile
tightened by his grin. He knows me

inside out. He's like a parent
come to collect me from a party
I've just started to enjoy. Ridiculously
punctual. *Oh, he can wait.* Yes, he can wait.

And he does, exchanging ghastly
benign glances with that corpse
of yours at the way we fret
over deadlines or how badly we've slept.

The Barrow

I'm thinking of him again this morning,
find him out in Tile House garden
got up in his creosoting coat
and that greasy brown corduroy cap
we gave him years ago. He's bending
over carefully to check if the roses
have been properly pruned, if the moss
on the path needs another dose
of Jeyes Fluid. He's looking for something
for me to do now, a few leaves
or fir cones to rake; not much point
but I follow him up to the gap
in the hedge, heading for the garage
where the tools are all hanging neatly
in their black silhouettes and the barrow's
propped on top of the tapering sheets
of hardboard he slots inside it
that double the load it can hold.
But he falters, sags at the sight
of his garage gone, what they've done
at the back – the extension, two storeys
that I was forgetting. As I do –
spending more and more time
in my head these days, keeping in touch
with growing numbers of the dead.

The Machine

In the daytime it lived on the window ledge
at the end of the kitchen, plugged in
beside the dark brown two pint jug
he kept topped up. After taking his pills
each morning while he waited for her
to come down for breakfast, he tipped
the night's ropy mixture of mucus
and water down the sink and rinsed
the tank and the clear plastic tubing
under the hot tap intently,
scoured the nozzle with a fine bottle-brush.

For four years he nursed it, monitored
its puttering engine. Unflinching
he sucked up the phlegm bubbling out
at her stoma, he smiled as he caught it,
he passed her a Kleenex, the ointment.
For four years he stayed alive
and breathed for her. She was my mother
and he – remember it, remember
how I even corrected the Registrar
of Births and Deaths, put her right
punctiliously when she called him my father.

Joining the M25

It was on the A12 going south
beyond Chelmsford last March.
He was stuck in a slow-moving stream
of traffic in the outside lane
on another visit to his mother
in hospital after her latest
operation, when it suddenly came
to him that he wouldn't mind dying.

He could indicate left and pull over
into a lay-by, turn off
the engine, the World at One,
and simply stop driving
air in and out of his lungs.
The children were grown, there was nothing
vital he'd be leaving undone.

Surprised, he drove steadily on,
only gathering necessary speed
as he joined the M25,
feeling lighter somehow, relieved.

The Scar

What were they playing, *it* or something?
Glancing behind him as he dashed
down the street he'd skidded on gravel
in the gutter and come a cropper.
At the sight of the blood, his flayed
knee, his screams filled the world.

She grimaced at the wound but went on
sponging and dabbing it, shushing him,
washing out the grit till he sensed
her calm and knew that it wasn't
too bad though it hurt, and that Dettol
did really sting like she warned him.

These mornings waking up in the dark
he sees her die, watches the blood
drain from her face
and wishes again that he'd stood
by her hospital bed the last time
she came round and somehow not cried.

Seeing You Off

Though red double deckers are parked
in all but one of the bays in both
of the corrugated iron hangars,
the depot's deserted – no-one else waiting,
the brick office locked, mugs left
on the draining board below a backfiring
Ascot like ours at Southborough Road,
the small print health and safety
pinned up behind a metal desk
with a calendar showing time stopped
last Wednesday, and hanging from a peg
a baseball cap, a lady's red umbrella.
Lost property. I check the framed
timetable and try to have faith, keep
chatting, read you the signs – *Buses
reversing. Danger. Asbestos roof
will not bear walking upon*. You try
for a smile. We could do with a seat.
I point out the ragwort flowering
between slack wire and concrete posts.
But suddenly it's here, changing down
under the railway bridge, an 84,
shuddering, blocking out the sunlight,
and now that I'm helping you on
I don't want you to go, to let go
of my arm, though there's plenty of room
and some of them I recognise –'El Cid'
rising up in the aisle and there's Gran
with an eager man, surely your dad,
and at the back isn't that Uncle Tony
waving one of his foul menthol cigarettes?

The List

Leafing back through my drafts for a spark
of life I come on the list
of questions we wrote out to ask
the doctor that morning. It's a shock
to be there on Elstead Ward
at her bedside again, locked on
to her uncertain breathing, worried
by the blood in the catheter bag
and the lax left side of her face,
not knowing how long she could last
or whether it's really for us,
the sedation we're arguing for
in the corridor – though she's unconscious.
We just can't be sure, it's a matter
of waiting mainly, Dr Clarius
tells us in almost perfect
English. I nod, add his name
to the list on the pad that I'll later
assume was a stab at a poem.

Afterlife

With the east wind clacking the cat flap
and the breakfast things washed up and stacked
on the drainer, I turn to what's left
of the chicken under foil in the fridge,
set a bowl for the meat on the worktop
and beside it my pan, the deep one,
for the bones – three litres – and begin
on the breast, lumps and strips, lick my fingers,
wrench a leg off, a wing, unpeel
wrinkled skin and add it to the pot
with the gristle, a tendon's white ribbon,
the hinges of the carcass that I snap
and pull apart so the whole thing fits,
the jelly from the plate scraped on top.

Not what he'd have called stock. He kept
an old saw in his kitchen to rip
through to the marrow. It's a thought
that rises to the surface, a bobbing
pearl of fat about to dissolve
in the soup I'm making: a thick
leek and potato, and later
in the week, if it stays this cold
and miserable, lentil and fennel.

Resurrection

You were dead already, I think,
that afternoon, coming and going
quietly, bringing us cups
from the hall to wash up and a stray
glass or two, sticky with dregs.

Now we're dead as well, we leave
the crockery draining and climb
our stairs for the last time
to lie at length in the bath
past thought, past hurt, only brought
back to life by the growing cold.

Getting Warm

Just back from a swim they're sitting
over breakfast in the garden getting warm
in the sunshine which picks out the pair
of honeyed wicker chairs, the oak table.
They've plunged the cafetière and drained it,
laid down their spoons in their bowls
and already the bits of core
from the Braeburn they've shared are going
brown and the pared peel's curling more
as it dries. They've fallen silent,
eyes held by the trees at the end
of the garden – may, chestnut and ash
leaves shimmering, shivering, beginning
to turn, to whirl, one's landed
in the cup of her lap. They're entranced,
would never choose to move again,
though clouds accumulate, rain
specks their faces, though snowflakes
settle on their hair and shoulders
and now at their feet a trench opens –
it's a yellow JCB, a pallet
of breeze blocks, brick walls going up
with gaps for the windows, eye-sockets
they stare through blankly, or would
if it wasn't for the ringing of the phone
behind them. He rises stiffly. She leans
forward, stacks things on the tray.

Nobody

If you can't bring yourself to build
a snowman or even to clench
a snowball or two to fling
at the pine tree trunk, at least
find some reason to take you out

of yourself: scrape a patch of grass clear
for the birds maybe; prod at your shrubs
so they shake off the weight, straighten up;
or just stump about leaving prints
of your boots, your breath steaming out.

Promise. Don't let yourself in
for this moment again: the end
of the afternoon, drawing the curtains
on the glare of the garden, a whole
day of snow nobody's trodden.

Rain

So much rain, such a cloudburst, and the downpour
going on so long that the children
won't be fobbed off, they clamour
for their boots and cagoules, they jiggle
about while we unruck socks, struggle
with zips, but they're out in it now, arms flung wide,
rain tattooing their palms and their tongues,
wading in the lake on the gravel,
while we're back in the pantry mopping up,
bringing buckets and meat tins and cloths
to catch the grey drips that keep tracking
through the tiles when the wind's in the east
that I said I'd get someone to fix
I'm reminded by that tightness in your lips,
so I settle to the job, shift stuff
off the shelves, clear the floor, the veg rack,
dry pears, wipe the spatter off onions.
Then later when I'm calling them in
for lunch, I find them squatting in the drive,
our heavy spades flat out beside
a land they've drained with canals
that connect and are linked to a sea
with its shingle beach where space
Lego figures stand waiting for a boat
to ground. Turning at my voice, they frown,
puzzled, as if they'd left me ages
before and can't make sense
of my English, my obsolete accent.

The Flat-warming

Because it was only a nick on the foot
that hardly hurt, she just went on
piling up plates and glasses by the sink,
slightly anaesthetized by the drink,
because the party had been a success,
because it was new, her first-time flat,
and she couldn't face waking up to the mess
and if she felt lightheaded, why worry,
she was young and happy, tidying up,
so it wasn't odd not to notice the blood
spreading, pooling on the dark blue vinyl
for some time, and though she was shocked
she assumed it would stop, started
mopping it up, just a vein bleeding
in the side of her foot, surprising how much,
but because she knew not to make a fuss
and had given up Guides before First Aid
and never liked 'Sternum' her Biology teacher,
because it was miles too late for her mum,
and the phone was impossibly far away
anyway over the new grey carpet,
because she wouldn't give in, lie down,
because she was strong, too fit to faint,
and tall too, five foot nine or ten,
such a straight column, such a weight of blood
pressing through her, that she bled and bled
and it wouldn't, couldn't, didn't clot.

Thirst

Baking in a queue on the M6 this June
somewhere, nowhere, near Birmingham,
you came back to me, 23,
in a white towel, wet from the shower,
stepping out onto cold tiles striped
by shuttered light. Italy.
Our first hotel. I could probably track down
the name of the town, but who cares.
It's your skin on the tip of my tongue,
your earlobe that cool drop's hanging on.

Awkward Things

Cutting the finger-nails on my right hand
Introducing her, not remembering her name
Another appeal in the post from Greenpeace
A fly in the kitchen
Lust and lack of it
Johnny Baker muttering outside Mace
The conversation at the next table
How Kay would like to walk faster and farther

Identity Parade

Hopeful of finding my penis
I work my way down the line,
taking my time as advised,
but gradually growing less
confident, more perplexed
by how alike they all look:
bell-pulls that ring no bell,
surreal pokers gone soft.
Might this one be mine
with its bulge of blue vein
or that one, shrunk by the cold,
skin concertinaed, a whiff
under the soap? Though the angle's
all wrong, perhaps my hand
would remember, could tell
if I'm warm. Tentative
I reach out, but freeze,
startled by the crazed
leathery back of my hand.

Close

Over these last few days
of black ice, iron frost,
of Tim going in and out
packing, hardly speaking,
I keep on finding myself
in that check-out queue again
behind them, my eyes resting
on the child on his mother's hip
sucking his thumb, half-asleep,
while the fingers of his other hand
twitch and nibble at her neck.
The woman, head turned away,
paying attention to her friend,
seems not to notice any more
than the glazed-eyed baby,
except that she hitches him up
and is holding him now, I'd guess,
just a little more closely.

Mending a Puncture

The boy's bent double in the garage,
he's hopeful, but the bike won't co-operate –
lying on its side, it jams its pedal
on the concrete so the wheel can't turn,
won't let him get at the valve.
The bike thinks it needs a new tyre.
It's bored with the boy's tight lips,
his feeble levering with the spoons,
his plucking at the inner tube,
and it can't believe how long
he's taking screwing the pump on.
With a faint hiss the tyre keeps deflating
as fast as he forces air in.
It's scornful of his panting, his sighs,
doesn't care what's happening in the house –
that the woman hardly ever comes out,
that the girl wears her walkman full time
and the yellow Allegro parks
elsewhere overnight now. The bike
just wants air in its tyres and oil
on its chain. It imagines itself
fizzing along in the slipstream
of a bus down the Brighton Road,
the shoppers stopping, mouths open,
the children in the passing cars pointing
and laughing. At Chessington Zoo
the queuing crowds let out a roar.
Growing stronger by the mile, the bike's
leaving Leatherhead behind, going on
past Box Hill, not planning to return –
it can't stand the mess the boy's making
with the glue, how he won't give up.

Permission to Breathe

It wasn't easy. He was still flying
missions then, navigating the Lancaster
accurately into the flak, into the foul-mouthed
shafts of the searchlights. Fifteen shaken minutes
from the aerodrome through the thin November dawn
on his motorbike and he was home. She was up
already with Tim in the scullery
putting the nappies to boil in the bucket.
Only one, the only one, he wouldn't be held,
stiffened against him, struggled and wailed.
It was tiredness, he told himself, tiredness and cold
that had set the tic going again in his eyelid.
Tilted by the child, she poured him stewed tea
and he took it to bed, warming his hands
a little round the thick white china.
Later aware of a murmur in the hall
he guessed she was strapping him in, manoeuvring
the pram, and he drifted off as silence settled.
At the Co-op she collected the butter ration,
at Willis' pig's liver for their tea,
and then she came home the long way round
beside the motionless cloudy canal
where only a mallard made vs on the water.
Tim fell asleep as they reached the gate
and suddenly limp from the broken nights
she flopped down by dad in the blacked-out room.
In that half hour before Tim whimpered
I began, though I was nothing to them.
As they slid apart, one of next door's hens
started clucking and mum almost tasted new laid
eggs for lunch – she'd ask Betty – but dad couldn't take
his eyes off the barrage pounding up
as they came in low for their final drop.

The Lawnmower

Irreproachable, the racket of the Qualcast
coming and going in the cool
of the evening, every so often
running on the spot while he empties
the grass box. This is the man
we've given up kneeling in the window
watching the gate for. So intent
on his stripes that he looks straight through
our headstands, our new backwards skipping.
Though the motor's died, the blades
don't stop at once. We keep back,
do as we're told, don't touch.
It must be overgrown now, the grave.

New Poems

The Page-turner

He sits in her shadow, keeps still,
as if he would be as invisible
to us as we are to him,
just his eyes imperceptibly moving

till the end of the page approaches,
when, rising from his chair, he reaches
forward, left-handed, and works
a single sheet free, then waits

for the moment to flip it over.
Pressing it flat with his palm
from below so it won't lift up,
already he's pushed himself back

out of consideration. Again and again.
Till the pianist bows, and he stands
apart disclaiming applause,
head down, holding the music.

Old Notebook

Sometimes there'll be a poem in it
that I'm ready to write now, see how,
however many months later.
And odd words I liked the look of,
pebbles on the beach I picked up
and pocketed – here's rigmarole, spooky, slake.
But mostly it's notes of what not
to forget, shames I'd rather not name.
Then Kay's wit, what I love her for
partly, just her words here – difficult
to decide if it's time to throw out
The Hellenic Traveller yet –
and I hear her, see her straight
face, the book still unread after
thirty years on the shelves we're sorting,
and we're laughing once more
at the students we were, those pretensions.
But here, on the page opposite,
Heather's youngest son, seventeen,
at a party, a little drunk,
falls out of a tree and dies
all over again, while I read on
that on April 26th,
up the lane beyond the black coaches
side by side in Shreeve's yard, I heard
the first nightingale. Which happens
to be another timely reminder.

The Door

This one went first when we'd hardly begun,
the son of the house, youngish, off for a swim.
This one had said she'd go early and went
without any fuss. This one was drunk,
a hand on the door frame to steady himself
before he lurched through. This one asked us
to hang on a sec, but never came back.
Nobody noticed the next one leave:
only her blue chiffon scarf on the arm
of a chair in the corner proved that she'd been.
When the door closed on this one I saw the light
in your eyes go out, and discovered my wit
had thinned, without him to hearten it.
Offended or bored by us, this one strode out;
and this one, confused to find himself left
behind, went hurrying after his wife.
This one went backwards, cracking a joke,
and this one followed with a feeble grin,
determined to speak out the next chance she got.
This one we thought would never be gone,
despite our exhaustion he wouldn't give in,
and this one went wondering why he'd come.
One by one they've gone through the door:
some without tasting main course or sweet,
some in mid sentence, some in their sleep,
some in sharp focus or hazy with drink,
but one by one they've come to the door
and felt a change in the temperature.

Early Morning Waking

He turns towards the door, the rattle
of a trolley or a bed pushed past –
not for him, not till after breakfast
which he won't get, seeing he's nil
      by mouth.

And he's hungry now, sick for home,
for a normal school morning – Joe nicking
the last of the milk, deadly flicking
with the tea towel, Sal texting Simone,
      hot toast.

Then the rush for the bus, he stands out
in the drizzle with Tom, won't shiver
against the post office wall with the others,
those girls. Tom brought him the hand-outs
      at first.

French irregular verbs for a test
next Monday, with another test due
that he can't bunk off or scrape through
by mugging up stuff at the last
      minute.

But he won't think of that, he rolls over
and lies on his back, a log floating
down river, slowly spinning, hoping
not to snag, to drift off, recover
      the knack.

Let him doze at least for the present
if he can. Soon the surgeon will remove
half his scrotum, which should improve
the prognosis, provided it isn't
           too late.

Now the waiting. He's fifteen. Not a story
I've had to make up. Any moment you care
to pick contains him. His thick dark hair
will grow back. There won't be much more
           chemo

with luck. The new shift's cranking up.
Someone passing laughs, maybe a nurse
going off duty. Is it any possible use
to him, to them all, my waking up
           early?

Living by the Sea

For weeks I've been on the qui vive
for a hint of a whisper, a footfall,
a password convincing me God's
coming through the lines. But no joy.
I'm dropping pebbles again
down the well of myself – still dry.
I'm poking about in this skip,
but everything I turn up's best
left chucked out. Good riddance
to the one true religion,
to the orotund voice of the priest,
to the boulder of dogma braced
against the face of my disbelief –
the Pope infallible on
and off, Christ's body and blood
somehow more than a metaphor.
And remember the rhythm method,
the self-flagellation, the Missions,
the solemn trumped up confessions?
Father, forgive me, for my sins
were of so little interest, even
to me. Thank you, D H Lawrence,
for Willy Wetleg. I'll miss
mass and not miss it, belong
instead to myself and this place.
Isn't the sea, say, sufficient?
Never the same, always more
itself than I could have imagined:
waves for some fifty yards,
beyond that, grey, lumpy, white crests,
a couple of gulls slide across,
black flags, orange buoys to mark
crab-pots that sink in the troughs,

a shag beats low up the coast.
Nothing else today. No boats,
the horizon a mile or two off.
Farther out I'd rather not go
for now. Though I'll swim, wade in,
the cold making me gasp, take
the plunge, alive and kicking
through a breaking wave's blind heave.

Offering

When did I last consider my heart,
pay it a little attention, honour
its sixty steadfast years in the dark?
Hardly notice it, my mind focused
on slicing an onion, on what I ought
to have said or done, the story I'm reading
now, Alice Munro, or remembering my dead
aunt Nin's laugh, those half crowns for ice creams.
Yet all the time it's working, beating on
constantly, like a god I forget
the existence of, keeping my blood
moving through its thousands of miles
of tunnels, making it still possible for me
to nod off after supper, to wonder
about Water Aid or no longer
postponing phoning my brother,
to nurse a baby grudge, fatten it up.
It's the size of my fist and weighs no more
than eleven ounces. If I bend back
my wrist, I can see the pulse twitch.
Millions of times. You can do the sums.
That's stamina for you, dedication.
Old squeezebox of mine, what do you mean
by your quiet insistence? What do you want
beyond the few lengths of the pool I swim
most days for you, and my sensible diet?

Patient Record

No heart trouble yet, not short
of breath, my weight still constant,
nothing but a bit of a limp with my hip,
here at the end of 2005 –
I'm writing it down, so I don't forget it –
this year you've lived through
with what your brusque oncologist called
fortitude, an unusual word.

Not Before Time

I take my dead aunt for a walk
down the lane. How glad she is
to be out in the sun reciting
the names of the wild flowers for me
again – herb robert, mallow, fleabane.
Even thistles and nettles excite her.
How could we do without them?
Where would they lay their eggs,
the painted ladies arriving
from Africa any day now?

Telling the Bees

Reading in this book –
my attention caught
by the photograph –
how the news of a death
indoors was brought
to the bees too, black
crepe ribbons attached
to the cottager's skep
including them all
in the family grief,
in case they somehow
got wind of it
and took offence,
went swarming off;
and reading this
I wonder what's
become of the pond
he dug and lined
and oxygenised
with a solar pump
for the frogs and newts
and dragon-flies.

The Shared Room

Miles away, most likely on his model farm,
driving livestock to market or pasture all over
the carpet, and Dad, from thin air, a row
in the doorway. 'Shut up.' 'What did you say?'
'Shut up.' And Dad, towering, yanked at his hair
and flung him against our chest of drawers,
its wooden knobs slamming into his skinny
shoulder, jarring the base of his spine.

Though he must have told me before – I couldn't
not have known, when we shared the bedroom –
yet it's taken me over fifty years
to hear. So now I'm kneeling, standing up
sheep, cows, his muscular brute of a bull,
reuniting a skittled tractor and plough.
And Dad, savaging his overgrown veg patch,
we'll catch him up later and hold him, 'there, there'.

April 15th

after César Vallejo

As you foresaw, it was in Paris
that you died, and raining too I remember,
though it'll be six grim years more
before I'm born. Today, the date
you died in '38, I watch you
playing hide and seek with Miguel
your brother, even longer dead.
He won't let on, won't show himself,
though you shout that you give up, yell his name –
peevishly lengthening the last syllable –
but keep looking. What else can you do
but check again behind the sofa, poke
the curtains, pummel the winter coats
in the hall cupboard, peer into the stale
crawl-space under the verandah?
You're angry now, your eyes gleaming
with tears you blink away, don't mind
me seeing in another century,
another language. It's not fair, it's your turn.
When you find him, you'll grab him
round the neck and squeeze hard,
wipe that smile off his face, make him kick
and punch you back, till your brawling
drags your mother from the depths of the house.

Fried Potatoes

Say the magic words and she's standing
interminably at the stove turning them
with a small kitchen knife
and that cooking fork Suki took,
its silver plating worn off
and its tines of uneven length bent
as if wanting to be her left hand
with the crooked little finger we couldn't
straighten, broken and badly set
years before she was our mother
by some fool of a doctor, a fall
at tennis did it or Zip her beloved
bull terrier tripped her? Stories
I never thought much of then,
being young and too full of my own
hunger even to know I was watching
the dollop of dripping beginning
to slide in the hot pan, to melt,
to clarify what it meant
to be her, here, all but transparent
with Dad gone off and us going,
cutting the leftover boiled
potatoes into slices that sizzle,
spit a little as she turns them over.
How long till they're done?

Oranges

Brought to us on a plate
at half time by the linesman,
we break from the pep talk —
he wants us quicker
at the rucks, more possession —
and jostle for choice of slice,
suck them, make gumshields of them,
or thumbing them inside out
we gnaw the last shreds of flesh
off the peel, wipe our hands
on our shorts, on Gorringe's shirt.
Our perks, our just deserts,
not given a second thought
as we spread out, take up our positions
for the start of the second half.

Down the Rec

He's nothing to us at first, some bike
going past despite the sign, a boy
riding round on the path. But he's stopped
now to watch – three and in, Geoff v me,
Jim in goal. I'm two-nil and Geoff's
in a mood, half-heartedly lobbing off
a long shot Jim ambles across for.
He punts it out and I trap it, tap it
forward, sure to leave Geoff standing,
but this time he comes at me hard, elbows,
barges me, hacks the ball towards touch
and chases after it fast, laughing loudly.
Then I notice the boy's got closer,
he's laid down his bike and arrived
at the goal line, half way along. Jim
ignores him. He's no-one we've seen before:
manky jeans and a superman teeshirt,
thin face, thin smile. Older maybe than us.
We know what he wants, that he's waiting
for a skewed one, a skyer, the chance
to sprint after the ball, bring it back.
And we know we won't know how to stop him
joining in, how the game will be changed
and how soon one of us will remember
the time. Cheers then, see you around.

Tinkling Cymbal

What I can't forget, better not,
is his look of shock, disbelief
at my cheery question. He was slumped
in his chair, no fire, far down
in the pit, on the rack of himself,
yet how sharply he lifted his head
to check could I mean it, and met
my eyes, his close friend, and saw
the distance between us across
his living room stretch, how much
more alone he was now I'd come.

Lesson

Five minutes, no more, our stroll
from the restaurant through the quiet
Sunday afternoon streets,
headed for our books, the next chapter
a bench in the park or stretched out
under trees on the grass. We were crossing
the Paseo del Prado when you noticed
my backpack gaping, unzipped,
the wallet gone, no longer mine.
Apparently it's always happening
with backpacks, but after the shock
and the hassle, it's the deftness
I'm left with, how I didn't feel a thing,
how you need to keep practising.

Algerian Iris

We lifted a clump from her garden
after the funeral, brought them home
and planted them up against the fence
outside the back door, where they go on
flowering through the dark months
like nothing else – fourteen
we counted last year on her birthday
in February. Diffident among tall
bladed leaves, the live mauve blooms
would light up her face and still do
for us: 'here you are' I say
all summer bringing her first
the saved water for the washing up
before it runs hot, and showering her
daily with our breakfast tea leaves.

Concert

The harpist – the scan's
confirmed it – has twins,
she knows it will show
soon, this evening, her thirty
fingers astonishing the strings.

Summer Arriving

It wakes me, 6.30, revving
at the window, intermittent,
a bee or a wasp, a queen
coming out of hibernation,
and there you are before me
with a handkerchief reaching up
to enfold it and shake it out,
wearing nothing at all
but light. And now silence.

Nowadays

anyone can do it, and you wouldn't
have it otherwise, like readily available
access to the internet, foreign travel,
contraception. You wouldn't, really,
even given last night after supper,
when despite you regretting having come
without your glasses, undeterred,
your host – a good friend and in many ways
a most admirable person – pressed on
you photo after photo after photo
of Australia, the blurred exhaustive tour –
'just to give you some idea' – of the rooms
in his son's new flat, the final straw.

Remains

What thou lovest well remains, the rest is dross –
Ezra Pound, Canto LXXXI

I've known scores of squares, wickets freshly mown
on playing fields, on sloping village greens.
I've clattered down pavilion steps alone
pulling a glove on or with the others,
loosening up, throwing catches, going out to field.
I've walked in, on my toes as the bowler bowled.
I've crouched in front of the bat and dived,
snapped up sharp chances, flung out an arm,
and, running underneath skied cover drives, watched the ball
into my hands. But forgotten them all, even
the dropped ones I knew I'd never live down.
I've bowled too, polished the ball on my thigh
and adjusted the seam under my fingers, made it
swing and move off the pitch. I've varied my pace
slightly and used the width of the crease
to alter the angle. However many wickets I took,
just two stay with me: Dad bowled for a duck
between bat and pad in the fathers' match
when I was thirteen, the strange pain of that;
and Clive Radley, then at Norwich School, second ball,
a slash at a wide long hop, a stinging two-handed
overhead catch for Crow Goodley in the gulley.
And I've been an opener, middle order, scored
runs, done my bit with a straight bat,
a good eye and dogged application.
I've seen off the pace men and learnt to play spin,
to keep the ball down, to cut and drive,
to glance and pull, to steal quick singles.
And once, playing for Tilford at home,
for half an hour I was possessed, I knew
how to do it and dared to, I drove down the line,

perfect timing, and taking the ball on the rise
I lifted it over the bowler's head,
then over long on to thud into the oak
and over long off to bounce in the road
and on through a hush, a storm of cheers
from the drinkers outside the Barley Mow.

On My Own

I don't waste any time over lunch,
I eat it in the kitchen standing up.
Bread, off the bread board – no plate –
with whatever's in the fridge, hard cheese,
some scrapings of hummus, a tomato,
a lettuce leaf or two broken off.

But with you almost always fresh bread
I've fetched first thing – a small
granary, an organic or a cobber –
I ring the changes, surprise you
with rollmops, an avocado, last week
artichoke hearts. And then, my favourite,
salad, in our wide open wooden bowl –
rocket, cos, webbs, whatever's
going or I'm growing, with cucumber,
olives, tomatoes, and on a good day
sweet chargrilled red peppers I'm peeling
when you drive in, still ragged from work,
and before we sit, settle yourself
by picking us some mint, whisking up
one of your thick mustard dressings.

Gone

after William Matthews

How easily happiness begins
when everyone's gone,
when the noise of the cars dies away
and you shut the door, turn back
to the empty spot-lit rooms,
the fire quietly burning itself.
And there's no rush, you can breathe,
reposition the cane chairs
in the bay, load up the tray
with the glasses and coffee cups,
not even caring who's
left theirs untouched. What's best
is this silence, not needing to talk,
your wife sent gladly to bath
while you wash up, no discussion
of the evening's success, no-one
expecting you to speak or at least
to make a face, only the cat
impatient for the Whiskas sachet
you'll squeeze out into her bowl
before you lock the back door,
and switch off light after light
till you reach the foot of the stairs.

The Man Alone

sleeps in a single bed and downloads porn.
It's not what he meant, but who does it harm?
He suspects the birds of a vicious campaign
to wake him at dawn, he needs his eight hours.
The muscle he's pulled in his shoulder fills
the whole week. An unintentional slight –
you running late for a War on Want lunch,
not phoning on time – he makes a meal of,
a bottomless cup. Of course he enjoys
his own company, but not these thoughts
he can't swat, can't stop copulating,
repeating themselves in his over-heated
sitting-room where he slumps in his farts.
He's let his beard grow – it's his dog
he keeps stroking, but out of control,
always rolling in things. He's given up cleaning
his shit off the sides of the toilet bowl –
the spiders knead the flies. He's sorry
for himself. And scared too now. Who cares?
He gnaws on the dry rabbit bones of old dreams.
Or unused to talking, he'll talk too loud,
gabble on too long to anyone kind,
overconfiding – his bout of d and v,
what he's cooking for his tea. No wonder
the Saturday girl in the Co-op's stopped
smiling at him and won't meet his eye.
He picks up his shopping, thank goodness, and goes.

The Tree

grows inside him, it's lodged
in the wall of the gut, absorbing
moisture and blood. He runs
rarely now, wakes up stiff
most mornings, takes longer
to loosen. The sapling's locked in:
it thickens, divides, side-shoots
grope for light and the roots
turn back on themselves and mat.
Already too big for its pot.
Hunched over, he seems to have shrunk.
Business, a grandchild, the Great
Wall of China, or just drop round
for a drink – he's more and more less
inclined to travel, to get out
of the house, of bed. His head fills
with leaves and the moist
scent of soil. Beech, birch,
box – whatever – he reaches
for the sky, the centre of the earth.

The Right Place

'Earth's the right place for love,
I don't know where it's likely to go better.'
— *"Birches"*, Robert Frost

You've fetched a duvet and laid it
lightly over the shoulders
of someone beside you who's slipped
unwittingly into sleep.
And drifting off yourself
on a sofa somewhere you've sensed
the same weight settle and known
how the warmth around you will soon
deepen your sleep. And that's something,
whatever else you've done or not done.

The Laugh

It took me by surprise, shook me,
bursting up from such a depth,
so resonant and robust
that I almost didn't at once
know it was mine.

As if it had come loose at last
like bubbles from the drowned farm
in the reservoir or finally done
its time, a prisoner free again
to stroll down this or that street.

Smith/Doorstop Books, Pamphlets and Audio

25 years

of titles by

Moniza Alvi, Simon Armitage, Jane Aspinall, Ann Atkinson, Annemarie
Austin, Sally Baker, Mike Barlow, Kate Bass, Suzanne Batty, Chris
Beckett, Peter Bennet, Catherine Benson, Gerard Benson, Sujata Bhatt,
Nina Boyd, Sue Boyle, Susan Bright, Carole Bromley, Sue Butler, Liz
Cashdan, Dennis Casling, Julia Casterton, Clare Chapman, Linda Chase,
Debjani Chatterjee, Chris Considine, Stanley Cook, Bob Cooper, Jennifer
Copley, Paula Cunningham, Simon Currie, Duncan Curry, Peter Daniels,
Jonathan Davidson, Kwame Dawes, Julia Deakin, Steve Dearden, Patricia
Debney, Mike Di Placido, Tim Dooley, Jane Draycott, Carol Ann Duffy,
Sue Dymoke, Nell Farrell, Catherine Fisher, Janet Fisher, Sam Gardiner,
Adele Geras, Sally Goldsmith, Yvonne Green, Harry Guest, Robert
Hamberger, Sophie Hannah, John Harvey, Jo Haslam, Geoff Hattersley,
Jeanette Hattersley, Marko Hautala, Selima Hill, Andrea Holland, Sian
Hughes, Keith Jafrate, Lesley Jeffries, Chris Jones, Mimi Khalvati, John
Killick, Stephen Knight, Judith Lal, John Lancaster, Peter Lane, Michael
Laskey, Brenda Lealman, Tim Liardet, John Lyons, Cheryl Martin, Eleanor
Maxted, John McAuliffe, Michael McCarthy, Patrick McGuinness, Kath
Mckay, Paul McLoughlin, Hugh McMillan, Ian McMillan, Allison McVety,
Hilary Menos, Paul Mills, Hubert Moore, David Morley, Paul Munden, Les
Murray, Dorothy Nimmo, Stephanie Norgate, Christopher North, Carita
Nystrom, Sean O'Brien, Padraig O'Morain, Alan Payne, Pascale Petit, Ann
Pilling, Jim Pollard, Simon Rae, Irene Rawnsley, Ed Reiss, Padraig Rooney,
Jane Routh, Michael Schmidt, Myra Schneider, Ted Schofield, Kathryn
Simmonds, Lemn Sissay, Felicity Skelton, Catherine Smith, Elspeth Smith,
Joan Jobe Smith, Cherry Smyth, Pauline Stainer, Martin Stannard, Adam
Strickson, Mandy Sutter, Diana Syder, Pam Thompson, Susan Utting, Steven
Waling, Martyn Wiley, Andrew Wilson, River Wolton, Sue Wood, Anna
Woodford, Mary Woodward, Cliff Yates ...

www.poetrybusiness.co.uk

Lightning Source UK Ltd.
Milton Keynes UK
UKOW04f1522060814

236458UK00001B/23/P